Wildflower

A Story of Resiliency

BY Janelle Hilland

ILLUSTRATED BY Justine Sarvas

Hardcover ISBN: 978-1-64719-553-3

For my Wildflower,
I hope one day I will inspire you as you
have inspired me. I cannot wait to watch
you grow and grow and grow.

All my love,
Mom

A mother and her daughter sit on a hill admiring
the wildflowers in the field below.

"I wish I could take them all home," exclaims the child.

"Well, then, how would they all continue
to grow?" the mother questions.

"I guess you're right," the child replies. "Hey Mom,
don't you sometimes call me your little wildflower?"

"I do," responds the mother,

"and I'll tell you why..."

Just like us, a wildflower starts as a little seed.

It is planted in the earth, not yet ready to be seen.

That little seed will grow roots galore.

And rise to become something so much more.

The young flower will grow and grow and grow.

Its roots like the family that you and I know.

This includes our friends, far and wide, who
will love and help us no matter the ride.

Be it wild and curvy or easy and smooth, they
will always be with us, no matter the mood.

As it grows, the flower reaches to the sky above.

The wildflower needs the sun like we need love.

The flower feels alive in the sun's warm rays,
like we do in the arms of a loved one's embrace.

Now I know this next part is not easy to hear,
But the flower needs rain like we need our tears.

The rain feeds the flowers and washes away,
All the dirt and mud and muck from the day.

Our tears help us to accept what we cannot change.

We may cry and we may rage.
But at some point our tears will dry.

And then we will feel better inside.

While the flower is beautiful, I must let you know,
that without its stem the flower
would not stand tall or grow.

When the warm wind blows,
the flowers move to and fro.

The wind strengthens their stems as
the flowers dance row by row.

The wind is like the challenges that face you and me.

Sometimes they are hard and difficult to see.

If we are willing to bend, the stronger our stem will be.

This is how we develop what we call RESILIENCY.

We remember that our roots will
hold us safe in the ground.

As we learn from the wind and the challenges that abound.

While the flower finds life in the warm summer light,
it doesn't seem to mind saying good night.

For when the sun goes down, the moon comes to say,
it is time to rest and put away your day.

And so, my little wildflower, I now say to thee,
we must leave the flowers to the busy honeybee.

Grab your things and let's go make lunch,
and always remember I love you a bunch.

I will help you grow stronger and wild and free,
so you can be the best YOU you can possibly be.

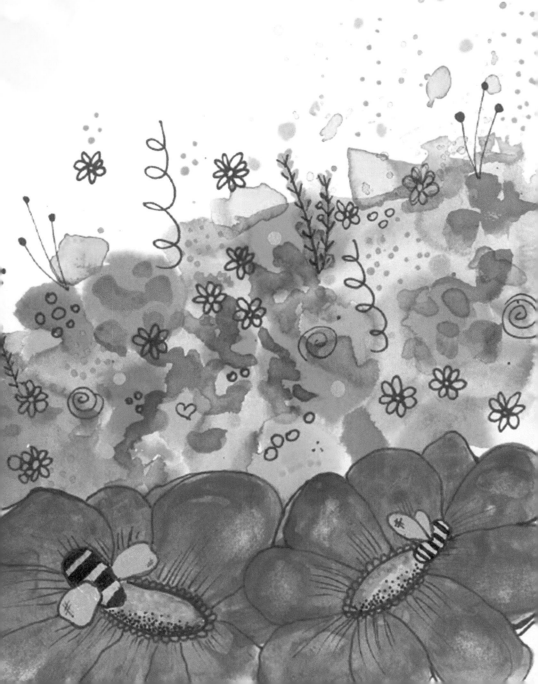

CPSIA information can be obtained
at www.ICGtesting.com
Printed in the USA
LVHW071647160521
687588LV00012B/715